# The ABCs

## ~ of Portland's ~

### Alphabet and Pearl Districts

Harvey Kline

*Alphabet & Pearl Publishing*
PORTLAND, OREGON

Production Editor    Tom Sumner
Cover & interior art    Karen Phillips (phillipscovers.com)
Original photography    Harvey Kline

Printed in the U.S.A.

Alphabet & Pearl Publishing
https://alphabetandpearl.wordpress.com

ISBN 978-0-692-74588-5

9 8 7 6 5 4 3 2

# CONTENTS

# PREFACE

WHEN MY WIFE AND I moved to Northwest Portland several years ago, besides falling in love with the city pretty much overnight, we were pleased to find the streets, south to north, listed in alphabetical order. It's good for new people and tourists. And one of the first things we learned about the street where we lived was that it bore the name of the "founder" of Portland. Moreover, historians portrayed him as a man of some mystery, about whom not much was known. Soon after that we heard the oft-repeated story of the coin toss which named the young town. I wondered if others whose names appeared on the streets of the Alphabet and Pearl Districts would yield equally interesting tales. Scholars have mined much information about this neighborhood from the days of the pioneers. It is not my intention to add to the body of original research on the subject. But it is my hope that, once in a while, readers will look up at the street signs and remember some of the people whose names they honor.

*A Portland State of Mind.*

# ACKNOWLEDGMENTS

I DISCOVERED QUICKLY that one cannot write even a short book like this without incurring a lot of debts. The list is long and begins with my wife Yuko. Without her patience and technical assistance this effort would never have seen the light of day. She spent many hours, snatched from a busy work schedule, answering what must have seemed like a steady stream of questions. I thank her over and over again for working with me through these pages.

For editing and all kinds of general advice I am indebted to my sister Helen. She smoothed out the rough edges in the text and guided me through the pitfalls of punctuation, citations, and more. We Skyped our way through the alphabet over a period of weeks and I owe her much.

For guidance through the publication phase of the book I tip my hat to Tom Sumner of Franklin, Beedle. Tom is a colleague from days gone by who has been an invaluable resource in getting this book ready for the printer. All of this would still be an idea in my head if it were not for Tom's generous assistance.

Along the way, I've met many others who encouraged and helped me with this work. Thanks to Scott Daniels at the Oregon Historical Society, the staff at the Portland Archives and Records Center (PARC), Meg Langford at the OHSU Historical Collections and Archives Library, and the Multnomah County Library for their assistance in gathering documents for this book.

Thanks to Karen Phillips for the cover design and art work.

For the second printing, my debt of gratitude extends to Ted Kaye, Northwest Portland history enthusiast, whose additions of historical content, careful editing, and encouragement along the way were much appreciated.

# INTRODUCTION

FLIP A COIN, NAME A CITY: the story that many Portlanders recognize as the event that gave our city its name. It's the story of two men, each wanting to name the new settlement after their own hometown. The guy from Portland, Maine—Pettygrove—won the toss or we would have been called Boston, the city which Lovejoy called home. A quirky tale and an appropriate beginning to a city that would someday proudly embrace the slogan *Keep Portland Weird*. The names of these two men, along with others like them, wound up on the streets of Northwest Portland in what we now call the Alphabet District and the Pearl District.

For some time, "The Clearing" had been a convenient stopping off point between the trading posts of Fort Vancouver and Oregon City, both already well-established settlements on the Willamette River. There was little evidence that the area that was to be Portland

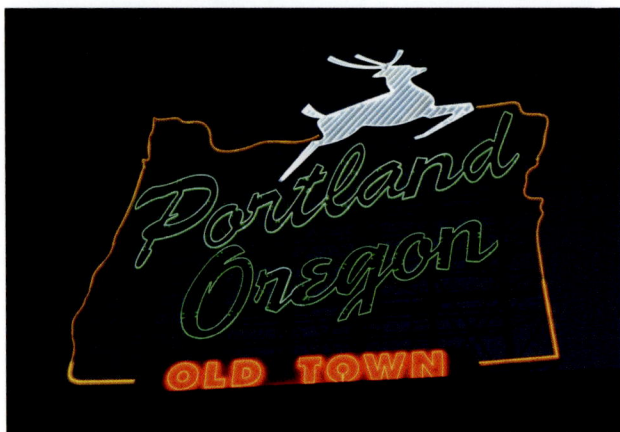

*The White Stag sign at the western end of the Burnside Bridge is the first thing that many of us see as we enter Northwest Portland. It was at this site that Captains Couch and Flanders built one of the first wharves in the city for their shipping ventures. The area around the waterfront marks the historic beginnings of the two districts.*

was inhabited. The traveler Applegate stopped at The Clearing in 1843 and recalls his visit at a much later date: "We landed on the west shore, and went into camp on the high bank where there was thick underbrush. No one lived there and the place had no name, there was nothing to show that the place had ever been visited except a small log hut near the river, and a broken mast of a ship leaning against the high bank . . . We were then actually encamped on the site of the city of Portland, but there was no prophet with us to tell of the beautiful city that was to take the place of the gloomy forest."[1]

As it turned out, in that same year the first pioneers who were serious about settling here arrived and staked a claim. Shipping captains followed close behind and soon determined that the location was better suited for commerce than others up and down the river. Portland was set to take off.

The historian Maddux offers three reasons for the first Portland boom. Opportunities for trade and commerce expanded rapidly as the California Gold Rush accelerated the flow of people westward. The building of the Great Plank Road (today's Canyon Road) made possible the transport of produce and goods from the valley to the city. And lastly, Portland was home to the first tannery west of the Rocky Mountains, filling a great demand for leather goods as thousands of Americans were on the move in search of riches.[2]

*The first planks for the Great Plank Road were "laid near this spot in September 1851." (The plaque is in the South Park Blocks across from the Oregon Historical Society.)*

In the early days, Portland looked something like this on a map:

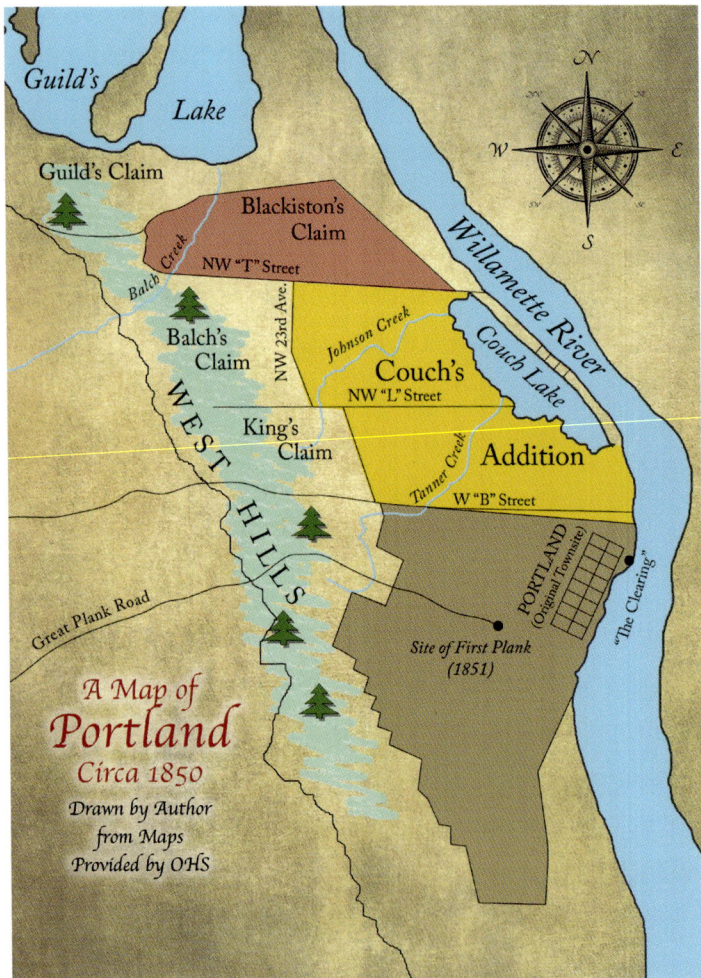

A Map of
*Portland*
Circa 1850
Drawn by Author
from Maps
Provided by OHS

Northwest Portland was bounded on the east by the Willamette River and to the west by the West Hills. On the south the area touched on the original town settlement and to the north it extended to Guild's Lake.

Much of the land was forested and as the forest was cleared, the stumps that remained gave the city the nickname Little Stumptown, still celebrated today with a coffee label. Three creeks ran through it and emptied into two lakes.

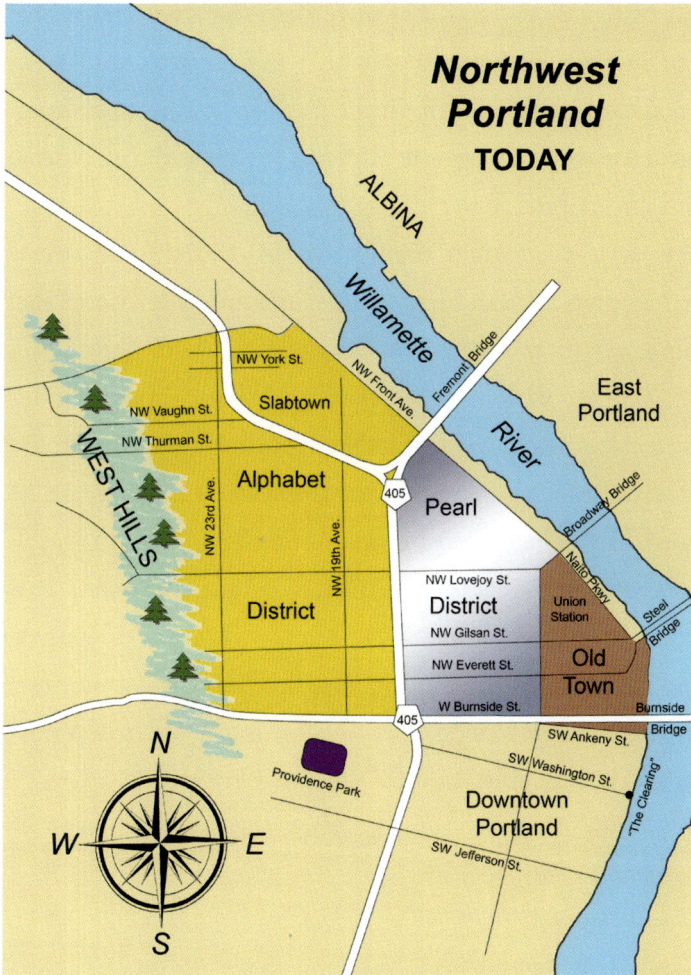

*Northwest Portland as it looks on a map today. The boundaries are much the same, but you will not find Guild's Lake, Couch Lake, or the three creeks. See Note at the end of the Introduction, page 11.*

Soon the land was platted, first into 200′ x 200′ blocks and later, west of 19th Street (now 19th Avenue) blocks were expanded so the upper crust could have more room to build their mansions. And build they did. There is an entire book, *Nineteenth Street*, which captures the display of early Portland opulence.[3] By the late 1800s Portland was listed as the third wealthiest city, per capita, in the world.[4]

That brings us to 1891. Up until then the streets, running south to north in this corner of Portland went from A to Z—well, almost to Z. But changes were in the air. Portland was growing and it reached across the Willamette River to merge with the cities of East Portland and Albina.

Confusion over street names was immediate and everywhere. The well-known Portland historian, Eugene Snyder, notes that there were no fewer than "twelve "A" Streets, twelve "B" Streets and nine "Cedar" Streets.[5] It fell to the mayor, William Spencer Mason, to appoint a committee to resolve this dilemma. The city employee entrusted with heading up this task was a man by the name of Douglas W. Taylor. His title: Superintendent of Streets.

Under his guidance the committee decided to honor "men who have been identified with Portland and its history."[6] We have been given no insight into the criteria used to choose these names, but we do know that there was competition for many of the letters. Couch had no rivals, but even Lovejoy had to be weighed against Lewis. Pettygrove and Vaughn each had four contenders.[7] And "S" Street was mistakenly named Scott Street for about a month, before it was changed to Savier.[8]

After much deliberation they submitted the results that history has dubbed "The Great Renaming of 1891." It was a monumental effort. The Portland Office of Transportation documented at least 582 name changes throughout the city on January 12, 1892.[9]

> That "C" street in Couch's Addition to the City of Portland be changed and hereafter known as Couch street.

*Each street received an entry that looked this.*
*(courtesy of Portland Archives and Records Center)(PARC)[10]*

Fortunately for the reader, and the writer, we are only dealing here with a slightly abbreviated alphabet! In Northwest Portland, the results are known to us today as the Alphabet District and, more recently, the Pearl District. The stories of the worthy men (and yes, they were all men) who were so honored follow.

---

* *Note:* When looking at the map of modern-day Portland, it might do well to go over several terms that are in use around here today.

In the mid-19th century, the streets in Northwest Portland were laid out in alphabetical order and ran east to west from the Willamette River to the West Hills. The streets run through both what became known as the Alphabet District and the much newer Pearl District.

Interstate 405 cuts through the middle of all of this. The area to the west retained the name Alphabet District, while the portion east of I-405 to the Willamette River became known as the Pearl District. To break it down further, Old Town is carved out of the Pearl District near the waterfront, and the northern part of the Alphabet District is historically known as Slabtown. Jane Comerford, in her comprehensive book on Northwest Portland history, dates the first use of the term Pearl to the late 1980s and credits art gallery director Thomas Augustine with the first mention of the word to designate the area. (Jane Comerford, *A History of Northwest Portland*, 78.)

# THE STREETS

# *A* IS FOR ANKENY

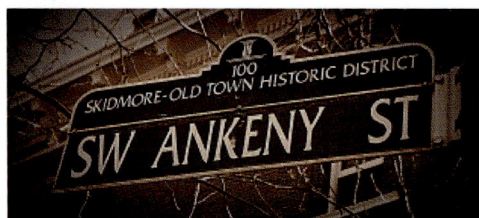

CAPTAIN ALEXANDER POSTLEWAITE ANKENY was a soldier, a miner, an adventurer, and the man who gave birth to Portland's market culture. He arrived here in the 1850s and made his fortune in the cattle business and later mining throughout the Pacific Northwest.[1]

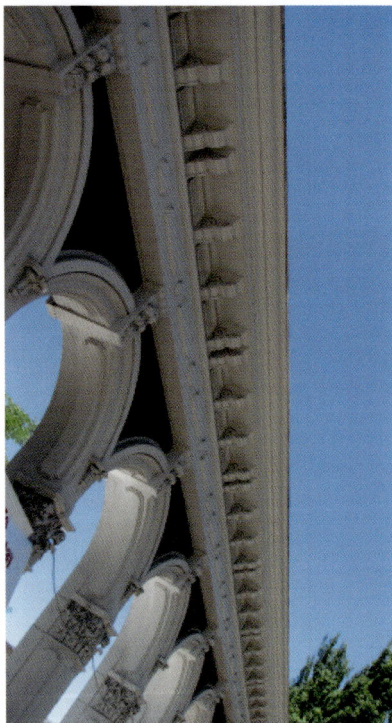

After establishing himself as a prominent member of the growing community he served on the city council before running, unsuccessfully, for mayor in 1859.

Ankeny had purchased some property on the Willamette River; he had lots of money and he wanted to build a market. In

*The arches pictured, at Ankeny Plaza, are the originals. They were salvaged and restored in the 1980s by the Friends of Cast Iron Architecture.*

*Voodoo Doughnut
has found a home
on Ankeny Street.*

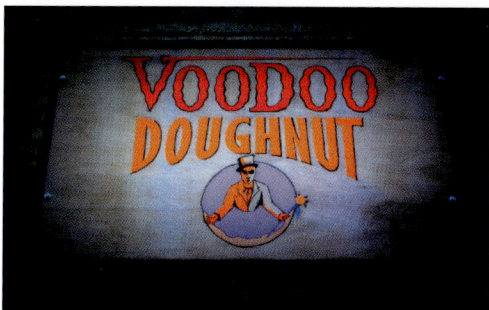

1872 he did, and it cost him $100,000.[2] The result was the New Market. It was such a magnificent structure that it became known as the Renaissance Palace, with a 1,200-seat theater, grander than any other north of San Francisco. The market had offices, a gym, a social club, and spots for 28 retailers.

The theater hosted General Ulysses Grant and booked a boxing exhibition featuring the world heavyweight champion, John L. Sullivan. The market remained a city social hub for many years, but as the city demographics shifted to the west it fell into disrepair and ceased operations in the mid-1880s.

The captain then sold his Portland properties and spent his final years tending to his lucrative Sterling Mine Company in southern Oregon. Ankeny died in Salem in 1891.[3]

## SW TODAY ST

Ankeny, the only street in the Alphabet District with a SW address, is a short and narrow street and a busy center of activity.[4] A vibrant market life thrives under the graceful arches that recall an earlier grandeur. The Saturday Market is "nationally recognized as the largest continuously operating open-air arts and crafts market in the country."[5] Look for several markers around the plaza that talk about the beginnings of the market.

Skidmore Fountain, a popular gathering spot (SW 1st), Dan and Louis Oyster Bar (SW 2nd), Voodoo Doughnut (SW 3rd).

# $\mathcal{B}$ IS FOR BURNSIDE

DAVID W. BURNSIDE is the gentleman whose name was given to this street. He arrived in Portland from Vermont in 1852 after a brief stopover in California where he searched for gold. He owned a flour mill where "B" Street met Front Street. He answered the call of civic duty and served for a time on the city council and as a volunteer fireman. But in an early version of "it's who you know" Mr. Burnside put himself on the map by marrying Jane Davis, daughter of Portland's first justice of the peace, and partnering with another prominent settler, Thomas Savier.[1]

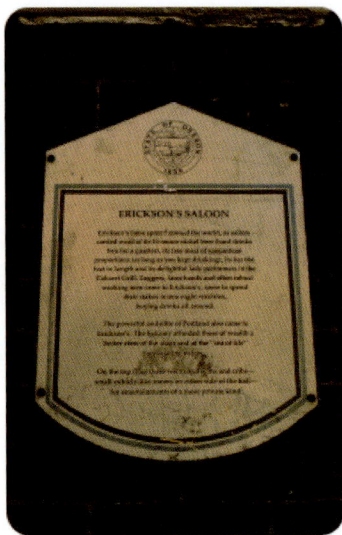

*The plaque is on the original Erickson's Saloon at NW 2nd and Burnside.*

Portlanders today know Burnside Street as a major east-west arterial that divides the city between north and south, connects the city to the east over the Burnside Bridge, and on the west

*Shanghai'd IPA from Old Town Brewing, NW 2nd and Davis.*

to the Tualatin Plains. In earlier times people knew it as the best street to get a drink and more.

At Erickson's Saloon "three hundred men could line up along its vast bars—one of them measured 684 feet. Loggers, railroad workers, miners and sailors poured into the neighborhood to spend their hard-earned wages there."[2] With good reason, Erickson's Saloon became the most famous bar in the Pacific Northwest.

It was from this "Old Town" that tales arose of men being "shanghai'd" to serve on merchant ships. And one can still tour the underground tunnels that spawned these stories and drink the beer that recalls its history. Ever since, Burnside has struggled with an image as the underbelly of Portland. Snyder notes that "this reputation was so opprobrious that it became almost impossible for an impeccable business firm with an address on Burnside Street to be taken seriously."[3]

David W. Burnside passed away in 1887 at the age of 62.

## W TODAY ST

W Burnside is the gateway to Portland's Chinatown and Japan Town (Nihonmachi), Powell's Books (NW 10th), Henry's 12th Street Tavern (NW 12th), McMenamins Crystal Ballroom (NW 13th), Providence Park, just south of W Burnside (NW 18th), Fred Meyer (NW 20th), Elephant's Deli (NW 22nd), Zupan's Market (NW 23rd).

# *C* IS FOR COUCH
### (SAY "KOOCH" IN PORTLAND)

CAPTAIN JOHN HEARD COUCH was one of Portland's founding fathers in the truest sense of the word. Many have argued that it was he more than anyone else who was responsible for the positioning of the city where it is today.

For starters, in 1840 he was the first to bring an ocean-going

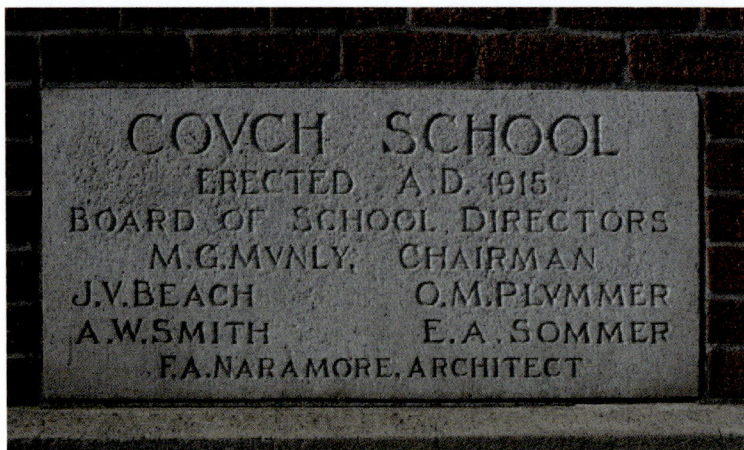

*This plaque at what is now the Metropolitan Learning Center on NW Glisan points to one of the many legacies of the Couch Family. The school is adjacent to Couch Park.*

vessel as far as the place that was to become Portland. With the utterance "to this point I can bring any ship that can get into the mouth of the great Columbia River,"[1] he determined that Portland, and not Oregon City, was to be the "navigation head" for the Willamette River.

That settled, he laid claim to a 640-acre tract of land in 1845 that encompassed much of the present-day Pearl District and parts of the Alphabet District. The Donation Land Claim Act of 1850 cemented the claim. When Portland incorporated in 1851 it included 154 acres of Couch's claim and made him one of the largest and wealthiest property owners in Portland.[2] He built his first house at NW 4th and "H" Street, on the west side of a marshy lake that covered about 40 city blocks.[3] The lake came to be called, appropriately, Couch Lake. He was said to shoot ducks for dinner from his front porch.

*The Couch house at NW 4th and "H."*[4]

*The house is long gone, but some of the furniture has been preserved and can be found in the Couch Bedroom of the Pittock Mansion.*[5]

We cannot leave the good captain without noting that he was married and fathered four daughters.

The following piece of local lore is recounted by MacColl: "How should a young man assure his future prosperity in Portland?" was the question. The answer: "Join Trinity Episcopal Church . . . and marry a Couch."[6] We will see that more than one pioneer took that advice and Couch's heirs populated the finer streets of Portland for many years.

*Captain John Heard Couch (1811–1870) and his wife Caroline.*[7]
*She was active in extending the plat of Couch's Addition*
*to the north and west after his death.*

Captain Couch was held in great esteem in his city. When he died of typhoid pneumonia in 1870[8] "the funeral cortege was never excelled in Portland . . . The banks closed . . . and all combined to pay respect and do honor to the revered pioneer and beloved citizen."[9]

*Trinity Episcopal Cathedral.*

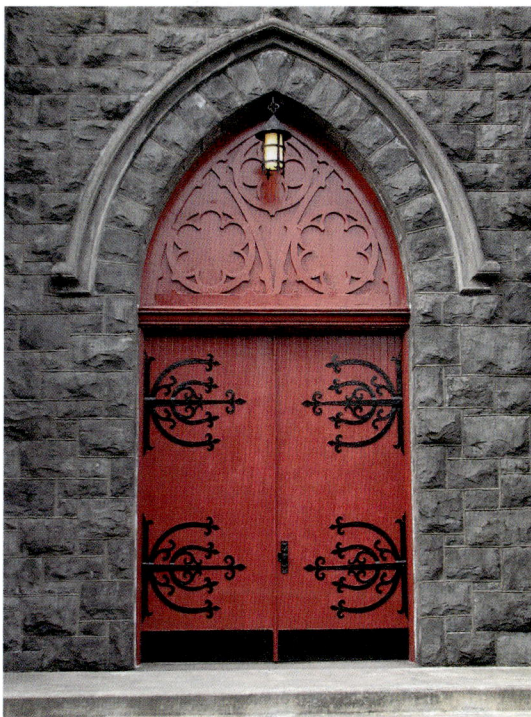

NW TODAY ST

Pearl Bakery (NW 9th), Sur La Table (NW 11th), Whole Foods (NW 12th).

# D IS FOR DAVIS

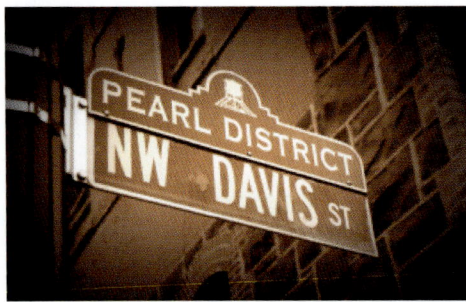

LONE FIR PIONEER CEMETERY is the resting place of many of Portland's earliest settlers. Information on the *findagrave.com* website for Major Anthony L. Davis gives us a good outline of the life of this Indiana gentleman.

We learn that Davis was among those who helped organize the first public school in Portland. "He was one of the most zealous advocates of Portland's free school system,"[1] and in 1851 he became its first director.

The first teacher appointed to that school was a 22-year-old Canadian named Mr. John Outhouse, hired at a salary of $100 per month. This was apparently not a living wage at that time, as he had to work a second job on the docks to support his family.[2] The textbooks he used to teach his 20 students: "Saunder's Readers, Goodrich's Geographies, Thompson's Arithmetics and Bullion's Grammar."[3]

Davis's service in the cause of public education and his election, in 1854, as Portland's first justice of the peace were enough to change the name of "D" Street to Davis Street. In 1858 he was also appointed circuit judge.

Davis's youngest daughter married the Burnside we met on "B" Street. A descendant identified Major Davis as his "3G grandfather" and placed flowers at the gravesite as recently as 2012.

*Anthony L. Davis,*
*1794–1866*
*Grave marker at*
*Lone Fir Cemetery.*

NW **TODAY** ST

**Gerding Theater at the Armory (Portland Center Stage)
(NW 11th), Deschutes Brewery (NW 11th).**

# $\mathcal{E}$ IS FOR EVERETT

EDWARD EVERETT WAS FAVORED with a street name for his activities with the Northwest Fire and Marine Insurance Company. Born in Boston in 1856, he arrived in Portland in 1883 and stayed. He was a businessman and a colonel who commanded the 3rd Oregon Infantry Regiment, headquartered in Portland.

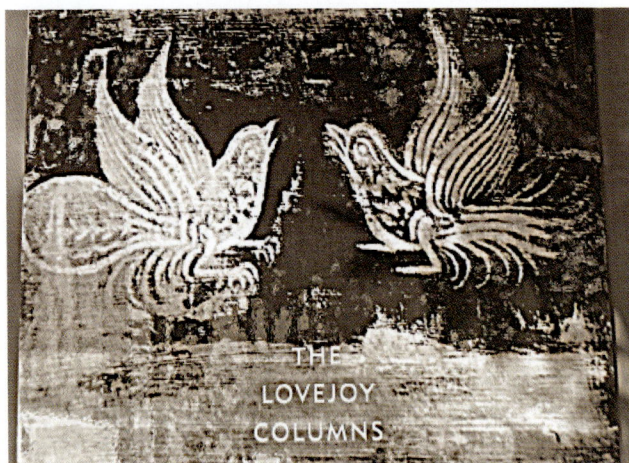

*The Lovejoy Columns at NW 10th and Everett were painted almost 70 years ago by a Greek immigrant named Tom Stefopoulos. When the Lovejoy Ramp was torn down in 1999, two of the columns were salvaged and placed near their original location.[1]*

In 1891, the year of the Great Renaming, East Portland and Albina were consolidated with Portland into one city.

In celebration of the event, Colonel Everett was at the head of the parade, still representing the 3rd Oregon Infantry Regiment. At the time, the modest colonel is said to have told *The Oregonian* that the naming committee had trouble finding a prominent citizen whose last name started with "E" so they reluctantly named it after him.[2]

When *The Oregonian* published its 1921 series on street names they said that "Colonel Everett, although not in the best of health, is still actively engaged in his insurance business, and is at his office frequently."[3]

*Lan Su Chinese Garden.*

NW **TODAY** ST

NW Everett is a busy one-way street and an important thoroughfare that leads east to the Steel Bridge. Lan Su Chinese Garden (NW 3rd), World Foods (NW 9th), Nuvrei Bakery (NW 10th), Restoration Hardware (NW 23rd), Pottery Barn (NW 23rd).

# _F_IS FOR FLANDERS

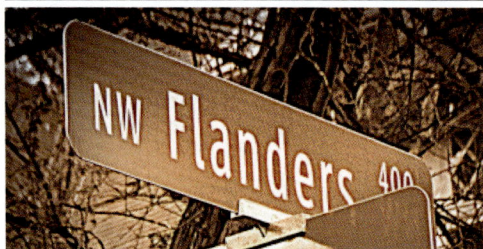

CAPTAIN GEORGE HALL FLANDERS was, like Couch, from New-buryport, Massachusetts, and he had the sea in his blood. He came to Portland in 1849 on a ship captained by Couch, who was by then

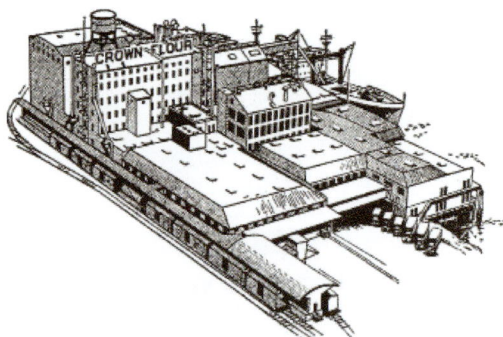

## CROWN MILLS

### FLOUR AND FEEDS

### PORTLAND, OREGON

---

_Centennial Mills, first known as Crown Mills, sits on the Willamette River at the top of Fields Park. It was built by Balfour, Guthrie and Co. in 1910, by which time Portland was already recognized as the flour mill center of the Pacific Northwest.[1]_

---

also his brother-in-law. They set up business together on the waterfront and built a wharf between "B" and "D" Streets.[2] Couch made his ship *Madonna* available to Flanders for trade between Portland and California.

And a handsome trade it was. Snyder provides us with an example, from April 1847, of just how profitable this trade could be. The bark *Columbia* carried 900 barrels of flour from the Columbia River to San Francisco. A barrel of flour cost $6 in Oregon and sold for $15 in California, showing a profit of over $8,000. Ships could make the round trip in about two months and the return journey, of course, also proved profitable. So it is not difficult to account for the rise of the "merchant princes," as they became known.[3]

*Temple Beth Israel stands on the grounds of the Flanders Mansion. The stone walls and the trees are from Flanders' time.*

Soon Flanders' wealth placed him squarely among the city elite. By the 1880s the merchant princes were moving away from the waterfront and to the wider blocks west of NW 19th. It was there, at the corner of "F" Street, that Flanders built one of the grand old mansions of Portland at a cost of $40,000.[4]

But if the sea provided his livelihood, Flanders' legacy is also tied to the rails. Those of us who go to sleep to the rhythm of the

*Steam Locomotive SP 4449, shown here leaving Union Station, is now housed at the Oregon Rail Heritage Center. The engine was fully restored for the 1976 Bicentennial Celebration, and is "the only remaining operable "streamlined" steam locomotive of the Art Deco era."[5]*

freight trains can thank the captain for his pivotal role in promoting the railroads. When it came time to build the terminus we know as Union Station, it was Flanders who contributed the largest sum of money. And it was Flanders and Couch who donated the land on which the depot was built.[6]

Flanders died at his residence in 1892, a year after "F" Street was named in his honor. *The Oregonian:* "Captain George H. Flanders is confined to his home by a paralytic stroke. His condition is critical and there is no hope for his recovery."[7] The obituary went on to write of the captain in glowing terms: "his was a character so pure that it was almost beyond human comprehension . . . a life spent in good actions to others."[8]

These virtues may account for his incarnation as the very good and pious Ned Flanders in *The Simpsons.*

NW **TODAY** ST

**TODAY:** Rogue Brew Pub (NW 14th), 10 Barrel Brew Pub (NW 14th), Chown Hardware (NW 16th), Temple Beth Israel, (NW 19th), Kitchen Kaboodle (NW 23rd), Williams-Sonoma (NW 23rd).

# *G* IS FOR GLISAN

(PURISTS INSIST THAT HIS NAME SHOULD RHYME WITH "LISTEN," BUT THE PRONUNCIATION OF THE STREET NAMED FOR HIM HAS LONG AGO MORPHED INTO "GLEESON")

RODNEY GLISAN WAS ONE of two doctors whose names were added to the district's streets. He hailed from Baltimore and after graduating from the University of Maryland he served for a time as an Army surgeon. When he moved to Portland in about 1862 he did two things that helped pave his road to success: He married one of the daughters of Captain Couch and joined Trinity Episcopal Church.

*Dr. Rodney Glisan 1827–1890.[2]*

*(Photo courtesy OHSU).*

Dr. Glisan went on to achieve prominence as a member of the American Medical Association and as a professor at Willamette University's School of Medicine.[1] He lectured extensively in the United

States as well as Europe and published medical texts that were widely circulated.

The memoirs of his sojourn in Europe entitled *Two Years in Europe* are still in circulation. Dr. Glisan's résumé included the first amputation of the shoulder and thigh in the Pacific Northwest.[3]

His medical skills were not able, however, to postpone his sudden death at the age of 63. He had participated in a meeting at Trinity Church and returned to his home at NW 18th and "I" Street in good health. Three hours later he passed away of apoplexy or "something of that kind."[4] Upon his passing, his considerable collection of books was donated to the library of the Oregon Health and Sciences University (OHSU).[5]

*Certificate showing Dr. Glisan's lifetime membership in the Library Association of Portland as of 1881. It cost him $250.00. "Before the library was opened to the public, only members could access the collection."[6]*

NW TODAY ST

Pacific Northwest College of Art (NW Broadway), Blick Arts (NW 11th), Andina Restaurant (NW 13th), Ace Hardware (NW 16th), Mission Theater (NW 17th), Couch Park (NW 19th), Metropolitan Learning Center (NW 20th), Trader Joe's (NW 21st).

# $\mathcal{H}$ IS FOR HOYT

RICHARD HOYT (1817–1862) WAS a seafaring captain and an enterprising businessman. He came to Portland late in life and died early in life but left his mark.

He had already made a career of sailing between New York and England for several years. There he met young William Irving, our next street name, and they later struck up a business partnership.

But it was the era of gold fever and before settling here, Hoyt stopped off in California. He found work sailing out of San Francisco. One such voyage is recounted by a passenger in 1849: "The bark *Toulon* was commanded by Captain Richard Hoyt . . . cabin passage was $80, deck passage $60 and it took 34 days from San Francisco harbor to the mouth of the Columbia River."[1]

When he arrived in Portland for good, he carried passengers on his steamboat, the *Black Hawk*, between Portland and Oregon City.[2] He later captained the steamboat *Multnomah*, the fastest vessel on the river. It made the trip between Portland and Vancouver in one hour and twenty minutes—about what it takes now in bad traffic! The steamboat caused much public enthusiasm and inspired this poem from 1851 on the occasion of her first passage up the Willamette River:

*"There comes the* Multnomah! *Success to the steamer*

*Sweet sounding her music, high floating her streamer;*

*The sound of her paddles the hills serenading,*

*And her smoke high aloft into vapor is fading.*

*There comes the* Multnomah *shout fifty glad voices;*

*Each heart beats with rapture, each bosom rejoices,*

*Her structure so firm, yet buoyant and airy*

*She skims o'er the waves like a sylph or a fairy.*

*There comes the* Multnomah, *we greet her with pleasure,*

*The choicest of welcomes to her is extended,*

*Because with her welfare our interests are blended."*[3]

*The Steamship* Multnomah *at the foot of Washington Street, Portland, 1853.*[4]

Later still, he purchased two other river-going vessels for service on the Columbia River. In 1857 he founded the Columbia Navigation Company which plied the river and tapped into the lucrative gold mining industry as far away as Idaho.

He was buried in Lone Fir Cemetery at the young age of 44.[5]

NW TODAY ST

**U.S. Post Office, Main Branch (NW 9th), Oba! Restaurant (NW 12th).**

# *I* IS FOR IRVING

WHEN WILLIAM IRVING ARRIVED in Portland in 1849 he was already a seasoned sailor. By the time he left for Canada in 1859, he had earned the title "King of the River."

Born in Scotland, he found his way to New York when he was only 15, where he met Richard Hoyt. He signed on to Hoyt's brig *Tuscany* and sailed with him between New York and England.

Once in Portland, he turned his attention to steamboats. He

*This home, built in 1884 on the corner of NW 18th and Irving Street, is one of several historic houses on NW Irving Street, which are part of the Couch Family Investment Development.[1]*

brought the steamship *Mult-nomah* from the east coast and gave over its operation to Hoyt. For himself, Irving purchased the smaller *Eagle* and put it on a passenger run between Portland and Oregon City, charging five dollars a head for the round trip.[2]

Irving may actually be better known today for the part of the city just east of the Broadway Bridge called Irvington. When his name was chosen to represent "I" Street, two streets

*Captain William Irving, Sr.[3]*

on the east side that were already named after him had to change their names: thus Irving Street became Knott Street and Irvington Street became Fremont Street.[4]

Irving's successful career in Portland did not keep him here for long. Within ten years he had moved to Vancouver, British Columbia, where he died some years later. His wife, however, did not forget Portland, and returned to live out her life in their home in the Irvington neighborhood.

NW TODAY ST

Union Station (Amtrak) (NW 6th), Ecotrust Building (NW 10th),
Irving Kitchen (NW 13th), Papa Haydn (NW 23rd).

# *J* IS FOR JOHNSON

ARTHUR HARRISON JOHNSON WAS BORN in London and came to the United States with his family when he was a young man. His father was a butcher who taught the trade to his son. The family settled in Wisconsin but Arthur moved on to Portland in 1852.

Upon his arrival he set up a slaughterhouse next to a stream that became known as Johnson Creek, at NW 23rd and "F" Street.[1] Johnson Creek has been rerouted underground and is all but forgot-

*Tanner Creek flows under this marker at NW 12th and Flanders.*

ten. Its sister, Tanner Creek, on the other hand, has several markers around town, most noticeably near Providence Park, the site of Daniel Lownsdale's original tannery.

Johnson went into business with Richard Perkins and they opened a retail outlet at Ankeny's New Market Building on the waterfront. "He was the heaviest dealer in meats in the city, with sales reaching $200,000–$400,000 per year."[2]

**A. H. JOHNSON,**
Stalls 26, 27 and 28 Central Market,
Dealer in all kinds of
**Fresh Meats.**
PACKER OF BEEF AND PORK.
Highest Price paid for all kinds of Fat Stock,

*Ad from* The Oregonian, *Aug 26, 1876.*[3]

Johnson later expanded his interests to include real estate and became a prominent landholder in the Goose Hollow neighborhood. He contributed to the cause of education by donating a parcel of land for the construction of St. Helen's Hall, an elite school for girls[4] and a forerunner to Oregon Episcopal School. His elegant estate and the surrounding buildings on King's Hill were demolished between 1926 and 1932 to make room for the Vista Apartments.[5]

Mr. Johnson lived until 1894, long enough to see his name go up on "J" Street.

NW TODAY ST

Jamison Park (NW 10th), Nossa Familia
Coffee (NW 13th), REI (NW 14th).

# $K$ IS FOR KEARNEY

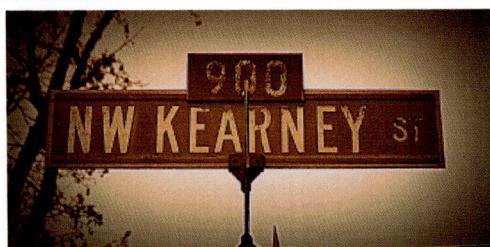

ACCORDING TO AN *OREGONIAN* ARTICLE as late as 1921, there seemed to be some doubt among old-time Portlanders as to which Kearney this street was named after. But most historians have settled on Edward Smith Kearney. He was a Philadelphian who was appointed U.S. marshal by President Garfield in 1881, at which time he moved to Portland.

His singular distinction as marshal: he sent the first three prisoners to McNeil Island Penitentiary which had just opened up in what was then part of the Washington Territory. Their crimes: two had been convicted of selling whiskey to Native Americans and received twenty months and eighteen months. The other got twelve months for robbing a store at Fort Walla Walla.[1]

But his stint as a U.S. marshal probably did not earn him a street with his name. Following his years in law enforcement he became a successful businessman; so successful that his occupation in the Portland directory was listed as "capitalist."[2] With his newfound wealth he contributed generously to the Portland Library and the Children's Home.

*The Oregonian* gives us a glimpse of his personality, saying that "he is remembered for a taciturn disposition given to eccentricities."[3] His will stated that he be buried alone, and so he was, in an impressive mausoleum in Riverview Cemetery, Portland.[4]

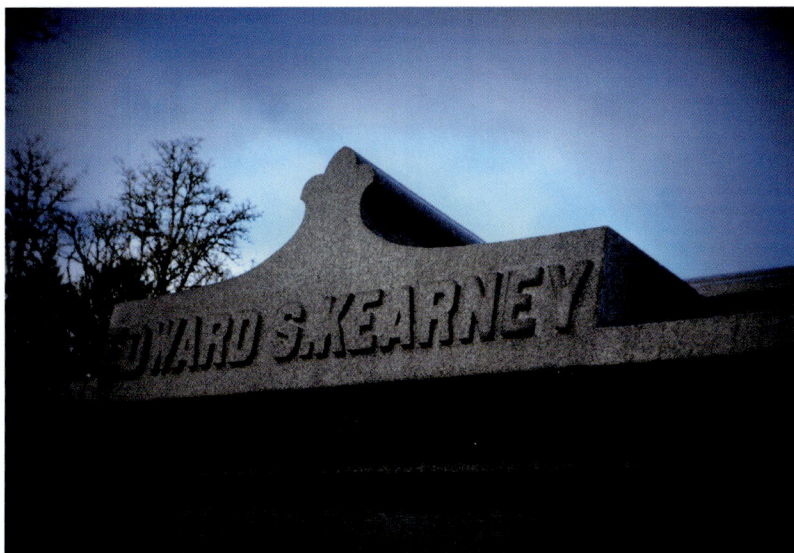

*Edward S. Kearney, 1830–1897.*

Kearney had a reputation as a tough guy and a tough enforcer. At the penitentiary he required his prisoners to work all day, every day, except Sunday.[5] It is no accident that he is featured as a bully in the long-running TV series *The Simpsons*, as we will see in the next segment.

NW TODAY ST

On Deck Sports Bar (NW 14th), Radio Cab (NW 16th), Café Nell (NW 20th).

# NW PORTLAND & "THE SIMPSONS" CONNECTION

THE SIMPSONS ARE CREEPING into the narrative so it may be appropriate to stop and pay our respects to their creator, Portlander Matt Groening. This etching of Bart Simpson can be found on the sidewalk in front of Groening's alma mater, Lincoln High School. The likeness, however, was not drawn by him as was first thought, but by another Portland artist named Matt Wuerker, in 1995.[1] Bart's name does not derive from a Portland street but the Alphabet District is responsible for naming at least four of *The Simpsons'* characters. For introducing these street names to a worldwide audience we thank Mr. Groening.

*Bart Simpson on the sidewalk,*
*SW 18th and Salmon.*

We've already met George Flanders, whose first name became Ned, the pious one. He says things like "Say your prayers, Simpson . . . because the schools can't force you like they should." And "I've done everything the Bible says—even the stuff that contradicts the other stuff."[2]

Edward Kearney, appropriately, became one of the school bullies. The bully's first name, Kearney, was taken from the street; his surname in *The Simpsons* is Zzyzwicx (pronounced "jeez-wich"). He is a bully because he's a Cubs fan.[3]

Lovejoy is next. His first name is Timothy but he is usually known as just Rev. Lovejoy. He passes on to members of the Western Branch of American Reform Presbylutheran congregation such gems as "Once something has been approved by the government, it's no longer immoral."[4]

Finally, there is the womanizing mayor of Springfield, Mr. Quimby. As mayor, his worthy quotes include the following: "You can't seriously want to ban alcohol."[5] Portland, the city acknowledged as the reigning beer capital of the country, no doubt concurs. Henry Weinhard, whose brew house on Burnside is pictured here, was an early giant in the beer industry. The surrounding area is now called the Brewery Blocks.

Two other names have less direct connections to *The Simpsons*. Montgomery Burns, Homer's boss, is a combination of two parts of the district—

*Henry's 12th Street Tavern, NW 12th and Burnside on the site of the old Weinhard Brewery.*

the huge neon Montgomery Park sign in the northwest corner (formerly the Montgomery Ward store), and Burnside Street.

And finally, the last name of Homer's half-brother, Herb Powell, is taken from the prominent bookstore, Powell's City of Books, that stands on W Burnside at the entrance to the Pearl District.

# *L* IS FOR LOVEJOY

I<small>F THERE IS A NAME</small> that is more familiar in Northwest Portland than Couch, it is probably Lovejoy. For he, Asa Lovejoy, is generally thought to be the first of several city founders.

It was Lovejoy who registered the claim for the land that was to become Portland. It happened like this. One day in 1843 he and a fellow pioneer named William Overton were canoeing up the Willamette River between Fort Vancouver and Oregon City. They stopped on the western bank at a spot known as "The Clearing." Overton liked it well enough that he decided right then and there to stake a claim, but lacked the twenty-five cents to file it.

Enter the lawyer Lovejoy, who, for a quarter, filed the claim in exchange for half of Overton's land. History agrees it was a good bargain. Meanwhile, Overton sold his half of the claim to Pettygrove. That left Lovejoy and Pettygrove to plat and develop the early blocks of Portland and, of course, to name it.

Which means it's time for the Portland Penny episode. At an occasion in the living room of the Francis Ermatinger House in Oregon City, Lovejoy of Boston and Pettygrove of Portland, Maine, were having a light-hearted discussion about what to name the new town. Their solution was to flip a coin, making two out of three "heads" the winner. So out of Pettygrove's pocket came an 1835 Matron Head copper penny.[1] They would each flip the coin three times. Lovejoy tossed first and the coin came up two tails. Pettygrove then flipped his coin and it came up two heads. "The Clearing" had a name. Lovejoy did not go quietly. After the coin toss he is quoted as saying: "We will call this place Boston!"[2]

But Lovejoy has found his honored place in Portland many times over. Besides the street, there's a bakery, a park, a fountain, an apartment building called the Asa, the Lovejoy Columns, and of course the beloved *Simpsons* character, Reverend Timothy Lovejoy.

*Francis Ermatinger House, Oregon City.*

*Asa Lovejoy 1808–1882.*

*(Courtesy OHS).*

NW **TODAY** ST

**Lovejoy Bakers (NW 11th), Safeway (NW 13th), Blue Star Donuts (NW 23rd).**

# $\mathcal{M}$ IS FOR MARSHALL

WE'RE IN LINE WITH MOST HISTORIANS if we choose John Marshall as the "M" Street namesake. Others who vied for the honor were George and Thomas. Snyder points to an interview in *The Oregonian* to make the case for John.[1]

John Marshall lived a long life, much of it on the river. He came to the United States from England in 1837 at the tender age of nine and following a brief stopover in Chicago, came west with his family. By the time he was 16 he was working at a machine shop in Oregon City run by Smith and Moffett.

But after two years he became tired of that and took to the water. Anecdotally, he is said to have refused to pay the $5.00 fare from Portland to Oregon City on the steamship *Eagle*, choosing instead to walk. He arrived at about the same time as the boat! He vowed to do better.[2] He first worked as an engineer on the steamboat *Enterprise* which ran between Oregon City and Corvallis on the Willamette River. In an attempt to beat his competition, the story goes that the steamboat carried a five-gallon jug of whiskey in an effort to recruit passengers![3]

Forty-seven years later, as the chief engineer of the Willamette Transportation Company, it was said that he had travelled more river miles than any other engineer.[4]

He retired in 1902 to live out the rest of his life at 827 Marshall Street, the street with his name.[5]

*Tanner Springs Park, NW 10th and Marshall, is a tribute to Daniel Lownsdale, whose tannery was a major impetus to development in early Portland.*

### NW TODAY ST

Marriott Residence Inn (NW 9th), Tanner Springs Park (NW 10th & 11th), Via Delizia (NW 11th), Bridgeport Brew Pub (NW 13th, Portland's oldest craft brewery).

# N IS FOR NORTHRUP

EDWARD J. NORTHRUP WAS a businessman who came to Portland from New York. A shipwreck on the coast of Chile almost cost his whole family their lives, but they made it here in 1849. After apprenticing with his father for several years, he went into business with J. M. Blossom and opened a hardware store known as Blossom and Northrup. The firm prospered and after several incarnations, Northrup brought into his firm a Mr. J. G. Chown.[1] Chown moved on to San Francisco, and there is still a Chown hardware store at the corner of NW 16th and Flanders.

Northrup often spoke of a Lt. Ulysses Grant, at that time stationed in Fort Vancouver, as a customer in his hardware store.[3] Grant returned to Portland after becoming a general (see Ankeny) but we have no record of him meeting up again with Northrup.

Northrup's story ends on a rather sad note in 1883 when he was still a young man of 49. While he was working in his Front Street building, he fell through a trap door that had been left open accidentally, landing 20 feet below with a fractured skull. He died within a few hours.

Northrup "was one of the men whom the community can least afford to spare."[5] His imprint on the young town was strong and earned him a street name.

*Edward J. Northrup 1834-1883.*[4]

His warehouse, built in 1858 and now known now as the Northrup and Blossom-Fitch Building, was the only structure in the Portland Yamhill Historic District to survive the Great Fire of 1873.[6] It stands on the corner of SW Naito (Front Ave.) and SW Yamhill Street, an important example of early commercial architecture.

*Northrup and Blossom-Fitch Building*
*SW Naito Parkway and SW Yamhill.*

NW **TODAY** ST

Streetcar Line from the Pearl District to shops on NW 23rd. Hoyt Property Management (NW 10th), Fields Bar & Grill (NW 11th), Les Schwab (NW 19th), Northrup Station Hotel (NW 20th), Paley's Place Bistro (NW 21st).

# *O* IS FOR OVERTON

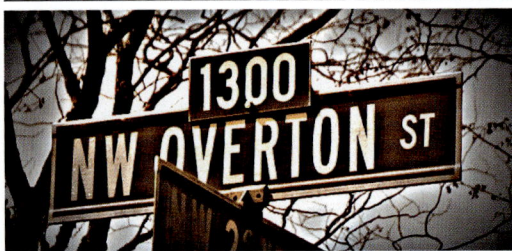

FOR A PIONEER WHO FIGURES so prominently in the early story of Portland and who is credited with staking the first claim on this land, little information has been available on William Overton. That is changing, as history enthusiast Randall Trowbridge digs deep into the life of Overton, tracing his roots to Alabama and later to Missouri. Trowbridge further makes the case that Overton's grandmother was of the Cree nation, and he has matched Overton's signature on documents found both in Missouri and Oregon.[1]

Earlier assessments of Overton were more dismissive. In 1875 Oregon Senator Nesmith is quoted as saying he was a "desperate, rollicking fellow."[2] Historian Harvey Scott offers the following: "This man Overton stalks through the twilight of these early annals like a phantom of tradition, so little is known of his history, character and fate."[3]

Long before Portland was Portland, Oregon City was an established trading post on the Willamette. Halfway to the Hudson's Bay Company post at Ft. Vancouver there was a spot on the riverbank known as "The Clearing" which had served as a convenient rest stop for travelers to and fro, and for Native American canoes before that.

It was on just such a trip in 1843 that Overton rested his canoe at The Clearing. His traveling partner was Asa Lovejoy. Historians routinely refer to Overton as a "drifter" but on that day he demonstrated considerable foresight by envisioning a town on that clearing. He told Lovejoy that he wanted to file a claim.

*One of the earliest photographs of Portland—1851 (Courtesy OHS).*[4]

There was not much to recommend the unfriendly site. Even several years later it was still being described by diarist Elizabeth Dixon Smith Geer in the following manner: "We traveled four or five miles through the thickest woods I ever saw on an intolerable bad road. These woods are infested with wild cats, panthers, bears and wolves."[5]

So for lack of 25 cents, Lovejoy, the lawyer, filed the claim on Overton's behalf in exchange for half of the 640-acre claim. Not long afterward, Overton disposed of his half of the claim to Pettygrove for $50 worth of goods. He moved to Texas, where some say he was hanged. Or was he? Trowbridge has found Overton's name on ship records indicating he sailed to the Sandwich Islands (Hawaii) and even returned again to Portland at a later date. History is unfolding as new facts come to light.

NW TODAY ST

Cafe Ovation (NW 10th), Fields Park (NW 11th), Pure Space Event Center and Table Tennis Club (NW 14th).

# $\mathcal{P}$ IS FOR PETTYGROVE

*Pettygrove (center) with his family.*
*(Courtesy OHS).[1]*

BY NOW WE KNOW Francis William Pettygrove as the winner of the coin toss. Who else was he? Pettygrove moved from Maine to the Oregon Territory in 1843 and worked as a trader. His trade was in wheat, lumber, fish, and fur, and his store was in Oregon City.

Soon thereafter he purchased half of Overton's Portland claim and set about to develop the fledgling town. With

Couch's backing he hired surveyor Thomas Brown, who laid out the city in square blocks, much as it is today. His wife joined him in making another early contribution: in 1846, their second son, Benjamin Stark Pettygrove, became the first boy of European descent to be born in Portland.[2]

Pettygrove developed a handsome triangular trade between Portland, San Francisco, and Hawaii and within three short years he became one of the wealthiest men in the territory.[3] He built a slaughterhouse on the river and sold his hides to Daniel Lownsdale who had just built the first tannery on the west coast.[4]

But by 1851 the California gold rush lured Pettygrove away and he left Oregon for good. His place in early Portland history is secure but he spent the last twenty years of his life developing another city—Port Townsend, Washington—where he died and was buried in 1887.

*The Portland Penny, Pettygrove's 1835 Matron Head copper penny in its resting place on the first floor of the Oregon Historical Society.*

NW TODAY ST

Planet Granite (NW 14th).

# $\mathcal{Q}$ IS FOR QUIMBY

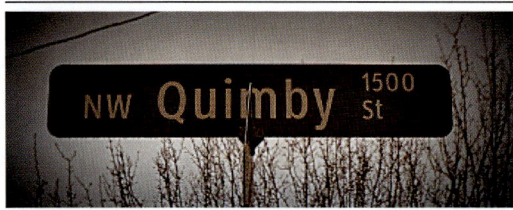

L{\scriptsize OT} P. W. Q{\scriptsize UIMBY} {\scriptsize WAS AN INNKEEPER} from Vermont. Like so many others, he came to Portland via California, stopping to seek his fortune in gold. For a while he was employed in the livery business. He did well and soon made his way into the hospitality business. He built a home at NW 14th and Johnson and he and his wife raised six children.[1]

By the 1870s he had partnered with a Mr. Perkins to purchase the American Exchange Hotel at the corner of Front Street and Washington. And what was a hotel in Portland, then and now, without a saloon—by 1873 the city boasted 73 retail liquor outlets for a population of 15,000![2]

In this excerpt from *The Oregonian*, the American Exchange Hotel was remembered as a "top-notch hostelry" which served "venison potpie." "Mr. Quimby in those days was a hunter of no mean pretensions, and it is said that he kept his hotel larder well supplied with choice haunches and sirloins of venison, obtained from the then good hunting grounds on Portland Heights."[3] And so was born Portland's "farm to table" cuisine.

He went on to own the Quimby House at NW 4th and Couch,

the best known of his hotels and an establishment which helped earn him a street with his name. It even had running water, albeit only cold.[4] A further description adds that the reputation of the hotel had "extended for a great distance on the Pacific coast, the service and accommodation being such as to delight the heart of the traveler."[5]

We get a glimpse of his personal life from this 1921 *Oregonian* article: "Mr. Quimby is still about and although eighty-four years old is seen almost daily. He bears the stamp of the earlier days with his Stetson hat, string bow tie and heavy gold watch chain . . . lately he has been passing his winters in Los Angeles,"[6] portending another Portland trend.

His reputation followed him to *The Simpsons*, where he is the owner of a saloon and the mayor of Springfield.

*Ad from* The Oregonian, *1886.*[7]

A Quimby descendant whom I had the pleasure of meeting still resides in Northwest Portland. Like his ancestor, he also winters in California.

NW TODAY ST

Play Date PDX (NW 17th), Bull Run Distilling Co. (NW 22nd), Wallace Park (NW 25th), Chapman School (NW 26th).

# R IS FOR RALEIGH

THERE IS SPARSE INFORMATION about Mr. A. E. Raleigh. His claim to fame seems to be his occupation as Deputy Superintendent of Streets—in other words, an assistant to Douglas Taylor, the man charged with naming the streets in 1891.[1] In an 1894 city record, he is listed as a statistician for the Customs Service, Port of Portland, with a salary of $1,400 per year.[2]

> *The Morning Oregonian* relates a good fish story about Mr. Raleigh under the header: "Fished for trout, got suckers." One weekend Mr. Raleigh and his Customs House buddy Mr. Forbes took a fishing trip to Skamokawa. It seems Forbes went far up stream and caught 30 trout, while our Mr. Raleigh and another friend stayed below and caught 60 suckers.[3]

Some records suggest that a second Raleigh—Patrick, said to be a descendent of Sir Walter of England—was the honoree. But his stay in Portland was short and his contribution was not considered of enough significance to warrant a street name.

There is not even a gravesite from which to gather additional information on this gentleman so we will have to be content with the little that we have.

"R" Street stood at the northern edge of the old Johnson Creek Gulch. The gulch, according to the informative book *Portland's Slabtown*, was used as an encampment for Native Americans until the creek was rerouted underground.[4] The language of trade in the early days of Portland was known as Chinook Jargon and this was one of several dictionaries in use at the time.

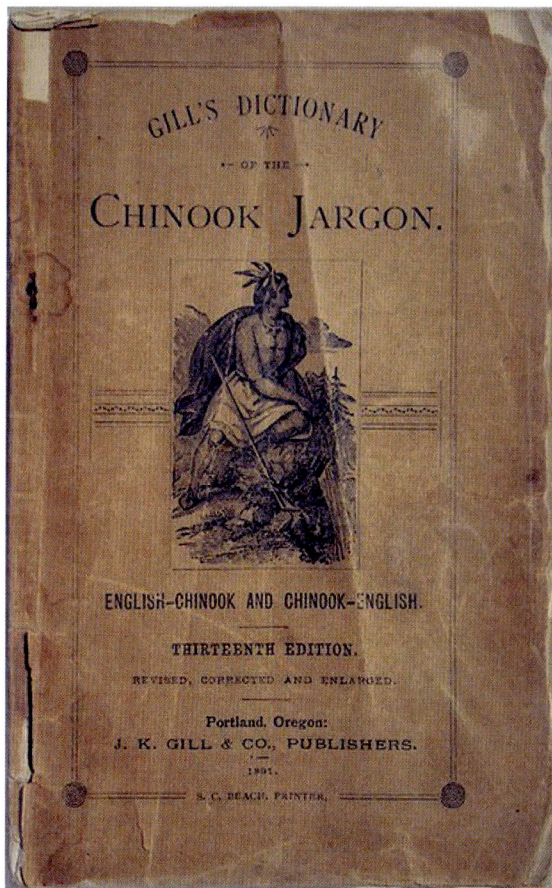

*Chinook Jargon Dictionary.*[5]

NW **TODAY** ST

Besaw's Restaurant (NW 21st), New Seasons Market Slabtown (NW 22nd), St. Jack (NW 23rd).

# $S$ IS FOR SAVIER

THOMAS A. SAVIER came to Portland in 1851 after digging for gold in the California dirt for a couple of years. His parents had come to Virginia from Italy, and were able to provide a first-rate education for their son Thomas. He went into the grain business with his brother before heading out west to seek his fortune. When he decided there was not enough gold in "them thar hills" he headed to Portland and returned to the grain market.

FIRST ORGANIZED CHOIR OF THE FIRST CONGREGATIONAL CHURCH OF PORTLAND, OREGON.
From left to right, back row—Capt. Henry L. Hoyt, tenor. Thos. A. Savier, flute player, E. S. Penfield, tenor. Jas. R. Wyatt, conductor and tenor. Henry Law, tenor. Harley McDonald, bass. T. Brooke Trevett, bass. A. R. Shipley, bass.
From right to left, center row—Miss Sarah Abrams, melodianist. Miss Leonora Bloreson, soprano.
From right to left, front row—Mrs. Alonzo Leland, contralto. Miss Elizabeth A. Failing, soprano. Mrs. A. R. Shipley, soprano. Mrs. Hiram S. Pine, soprano. Mrs. A. E. Chamberlain, soprano. Miss Helen Burton, soprano.

*First Choir of the First Congregational Church of Portland, Oregon; Thomas Savier, flute player, back row, second from left.*[1]

Savier worked in a general store on the waterfront before entering into a partnership with the owner. After the owner's death, he and Mr. Burnside got together to purchase the business, paying the tidy sum of $120,000.[2]

He had found his gold in grain. Together they prospered and expanded into the international shipping business. Over the next 25 years Savier and his partner built a fleet of ships which sailed the seven seas. Upon his death in 1876, he left behind a thriving company and a street with his name.

*From 1/2/1892 to 2/5/1892 "S" Street was named Scott Street. This document, signed by Mayor W. S. Mason, changes the name to Savier Street.[3] Snyder notes that Scott was one of the names under consideration for "S" Street.*

A recent *NW Examiner* carried an obituary for Henry Savier Mears, Jr., age 94, the great-grandson of Thomas Savier,[4] making this history a little less remote.

NW **TODAY** ST

**U.S. Post Office, Forest Park Branch (NW 24th).**

# *T* IS FOR THURMAN

G. William Thurman's contribution to Portland was his work as an assistant manager of the Pacific Postal Telegraph Cable Company. He was no doubt very good at his job but it was probably his friendship with Douglas Taylor that got him a street with his name on it. You will remember Mr. Taylor as the man in charge of naming streets, so we can put yet another street in the "who you know" category. Taylor, in fact, may well have resisted putting his own name on "T" Street! SW Taylor Street in downtown Portland was named for President Zachary Taylor.[1]

*An occasional horse can still be found tied up to one of old rings around Portland This one was on NW Quimby.*

It seems that there was actually some doubt over which Thurman was so honored. *The Oregonian* series on street names from 1921, after naming some of the Thurmans who had lived in Portland, concludes: "Men well informed in the history and the early citizenry of Portland are unable to recall the man for whom

T street was renamed and the doubt which now exists regarding the name of Thurman Street bids well to be permanent."[2]

It was left to Snyder's comprehensive work on the subject in 1972 to give the nod to the aforementioned G. William Thurman.

In the more recent past, famed novelist and longtime Thurman Street resident Ursula K. Le Guin wrote *Blue Moon over Thurman Street* in 1994.

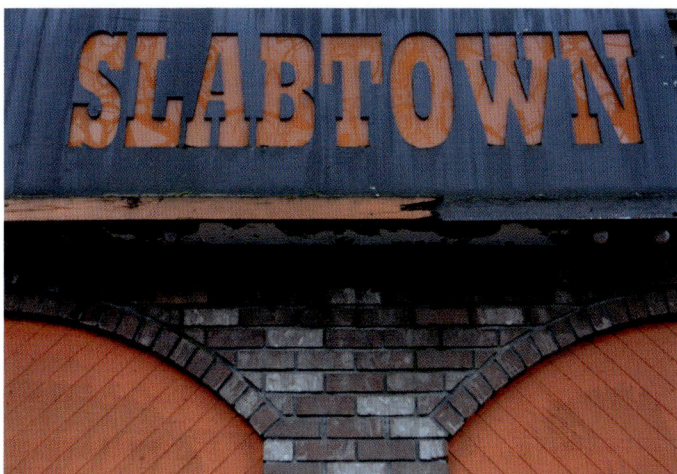

*The Slabtown Bar at NW 16th and Marshall closed after a 2015 fire and has since been demolished. Slabtown does not figure in the naming of our streets, but many of these streets run through this historic neighborhood within the Alphabet District.*[3]

## NW TODAY ST

Smith Teamaker (NW 17th), Cash and Carry (NW 19th), Multnomah County Library—Northwest Branch (NW 23rd), St. Honoré Bakery (NW 23rd), Food Front Coop (NW 23rd Pl.), Friendly House (NW 26th).

# *U* IS FOR UPSHUR

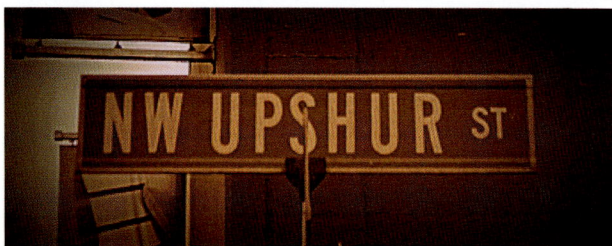

ABEL PARKER UPSHUR, 1790–1844, was a national figure and the only alphabet street name honoree never to set foot in Portland. In 1843 he had succeeded Daniel Webster as secretary of state under President Tyler. A conservative Virginian, he had no personal ties to the Oregon Territory. He did, however, hold strong positions on the westward expansion of the United States. He advocated for the entry of Texas into the United States as a slave state, and pushed for Oregon's statehood.[1]

An unfortunate turn of events kept Secretary of State Upshur from welcoming Oregon into in the Union as the 33rd state in 1859. In 1844 he had been invited, along with President Tyler, to observe the firing of a cannon on the newly launched

*Abel Parker Upshur, secretary of state.*[2]

*Explosion of the long gun the* Peacemaker
*on board the USS* Princeton, *1844.*[4]

USS *Princeton.* One of the long guns, (mis)labeled the *Peacemaker*, and the second cannon, the *Oregon,* were at the time the navy's longest guns.[3]

In short, the *Peacemaker* misfired, killing Upshur and five other dignitaries in attendance. The president was below deck at the time. For Upshur's efforts on behalf of the Oregon Territory, "U" Street was named in his honor; or perhaps it was because no other prominent pioneer names began with this unusual letter.

NW **TODAY** ST

Globe Lighting Supply (NW 19th).

# *V* IS FOR VAUGHN

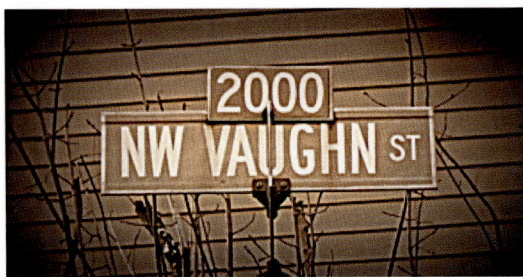

SEVERAL POLITICIANS HAD THEIR NAMES placed onto Alphabet District streets, but only one Portland mayor—with the imposing name of George Washington Vaughn. He was mayor only briefly (1855–56) and made his considerable wealth in various commercial enterprises.

Vaughn partnered with Captain Ankeny to run boats on the river, and he owned a hardware store and the first steam mill in Portland. Both buildings were destroyed in the Great Fire of 1873. The fire deserves a brief mention here, though it has been thoroughly documented in various histories, most recently in Dan Haneckow's excellent blog *Café Unknown*.[1]

*The Oregonian* dramatized the fire thusly: "And lo! From the bosom of the city a slender spire of flames."[2] The former Mayor Vaughn's mill, worth $150,000, sustained the greatest damage and was insured for only $6,000.[3] The paper noted that the losses did not "leave him insolvent, and he was in good shape financially when he died on March 4, 1877."[4]

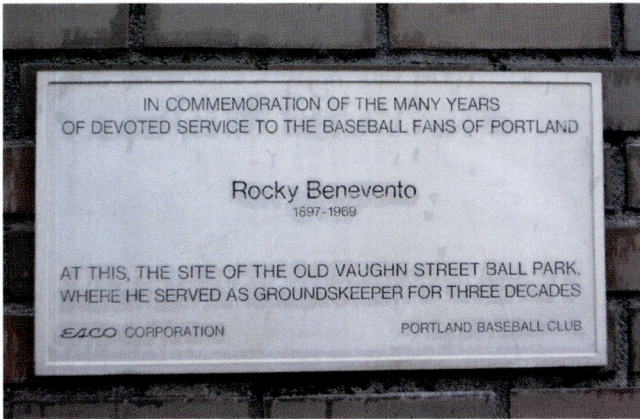

*Plaque honoring Rocky Benevento, long time groundskeeper at the Vaughn Street Ball Park, NW 24th and Vaughn.*

To the dwindling number of baseball lovers in Portland, Vaughn Street will always recall the Vaughn Street Ball Park, original home of the Portland Beavers. It's where Slabtown's Johnny Pesky, Mr. Red Sox, honed his skills, and Satchel Paige, Ted Williams, and Portland's own Mickey Lolich made appearances.[5]

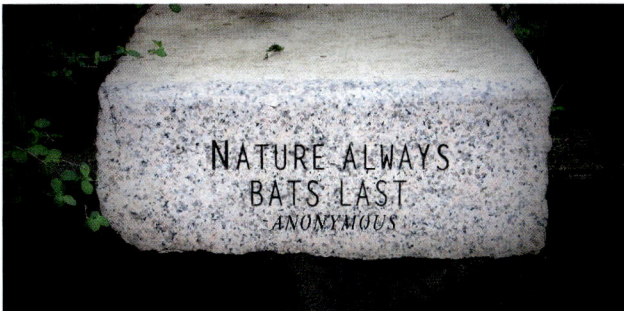

*Portland's take on baseball.*

### NW TODAY ST

**Esco Corporation (NW 24th) at the site of the old ball park, Meriwether's Restaurant (NW 26th), Montgomery Park (NW 27th).**

# $\mathcal{W}$ IS FOR WILSON

D<small>R</small>. R. B. W<small>ILSON IS THE SECOND DOCTOR</small> to be dignified with a street name. He preceded Dr. Glisan and is hailed by the historian Gaston as "the first physician of distinguished ability and education to settle and grow with the city."[1] Early on he alerted the city council to an outbreak of smallpox which led to some extraordinary measures aimed at containing it. One council motion required that "a flag twenty-one feet square shall float over each house in which the smallpox exists."[2]

He was a member of the original staff of Good Samaritan Hospital. Along with Dr. Glisan, his book collection became the foundation for the original OHSU library, which was known as the R. B. Wilson Library from 1893 to 1919.[3]

*Dr. Robert B. Wilson 1828–1877.*[4]
*(Photo courtesy of OHSU.)*

64

*Willamette University Medical Department, 1889,*
*NW 15th & "C" Street, a forerunner of OHSU.*[5]
*The building was later used as the College of Dentistry and Pharmacy.*
*(Photo courtesy of OHSU.)*

He arrived in Portland, not unusually, after a gold digging stint in California. But more unusually, he then became the ship doctor on the aptly named steamer, *Gold Hunter*, which carried goods and passengers between San Francisco and Portland. By late 1850 he decided not to return to the land of gold.

Instead, he remained here and married Captain Couch's eldest daughter, Caroline, thus setting in motion the oft-quoted advice about getting ahead in Portland.

Dr. Wilson succumbed to pneumonia in 1877. He left behind seven children, two of whom became prominent Portland physicians.[6]

NW TODAY ST

Clear Creek Distillery (NW 24th).

# *Y* IS FOR YORK

*AUTHOR'S NOTE: The street name's the same. The people honored are very different. Earlier writers had speculated that the street was named after the Rev. John York or a confectioner named Milton York. The man honored today was a slave known only as York.*

*As Portland prepared to commemorate the 2003–2006 bicentennial of the Lewis & Clark Expedition, the local planning group associated with the Oregon Historical Society (Lewis & Clark 2005) learned that the namesake of York Street was unknown. So it asked the city to declare that the "Y" Street be thereafter named for William Clark's slave, York.[1] Thus in 2002, the Portland City Council, with Mayor Vera Katz presiding, passed Resolution No. 36070 directing the Department of Transportation to record that the street honors York for "his role in the Lewis & Clark Expedition and the history of the City of Portland," making NW York Street the first street in the nation to do so.[2]*

WHAT DO WE KNOW about Clark's slave York and what were his particular contributions to Portland's history? To begin at the journey's end, York was a member of William Clark's small exploration party, which canoed up the Willamette River to the vicinity of today's St. John's Bridge in April, 1806, thus making him among the first explorers to paddle around present day Portland. By this time the historic expedition had already reached the Pacific Ocean, and York had become the first African-American man to cross the continent north of Mexico.[3] These facts alone are enough to secure his place in Portland's history.

Much has been written about the curiosity with which Native Americans viewed York. They wanted to rub the paint off his skin, they attributed magical powers to him and called him "medicine man," and at times they were in awe of his strength and stature.

But York's contributions were far more than skin deep. Along the way and in all respects he proved to be a valuable member of the expedition. He carried a rifle, he hunted and scouted,

York as depicted in an eight story–high trompe l'oeil mural on the Oregon Historical Society's building, painted in 1989 by noted artist Richard Haas. The mural also depicts Lewis, Clark, Sacagawea, and the dog Seaman.

and he was entrusted to trade on behalf of the expedition. When the Corps of Discovery, as they were known, reached the Pacific Ocean and chose Fort Clatsop as the place to spend the winter, York was consulted as an equal member of the group and his vote was counted with the others. It was likely the first vote ever cast by an African-American slave.

Yet, for all his skills and accomplishments, York remained a slave. As Clark later wrote his brother: "I gave him a Severe trouncing the other Day and he has much mended Sence."[5] And when the expedition got back to St. Louis in 1806 and others were rewarded with double pay and land grants, York continued to live in slavery, until Clark freed him many years later.[6] By 1832, Clark reported the death of York by cholera.

Portland filmmaker Ron Craig, in his award-winning documentary *The Undiscovered Explorer: Imagining York*, seeks to give voice to this heroic, yet tragic figure from our history, saying: "My goal is to take him where he couldn't go when he was alive."[7] The new York's name on "Y" Street is a small step in that direction.

OFFICIAL MAILING CARD
CLARK CENTENNIAL 1905
PORTLAND, OREGON.

FORESTRY BUILDING.

PUBLISHED BY B.B. RICH, OFFICIAL STATIONER

*The Forestry Building, an exhibition hall showcasing the timber industry at the 1905 Lewis & Clark Exposition, was said to be largest log cabin in the world. It burned to the ground in a spectacular fire in 1964.*

*One hundred years after the Lewis & Clark Expedition, and not far from York Street in NW Portland, the 1905 Lewis & Clark Centennial Exposition marked the end of the old and the beginning of the new Oregon.[8] Portland closed the chapter on its pioneering days and heralded the birth of the city as we know it today. The Exposition lasted about five months and showcased exhibits from 21 countries and 16 states.[9] The physical traces of the expedition have vanished but the economic impact was strong and lasting. Portland, in short, had entered the modern era and gained a worldwide audience.*

*And 200 years after the Lewis & Clark Expedition, a forward-looking Bicentennial group reached into the past and rededicated NW York Street in honor of a slave who had played such a significant role in the early explorations of Portland.*

# POSTSCRIPT

WE HAVE COME TO THE END of the Great Renaming of 1891 but, of course, not quite to the end of the alphabet. Mr. Taylor apparently could not find two worthy citizens whose names began with X and Z.

So instead, "X" Street eventually became Roosevelt and was so named in 1903 for President Theodore Roosevelt.[1] Roosevelt was the president at the time of the 1905 Lewis & Clark Exposition and he sent his vice president, Charles Fairbanks, to open the Exposition.[2] "Z" Street had already been named Reed Street in 1883 in honor of Simeon and Amanda Reed, later the benefactors of Reed College, and the name remained.[3]

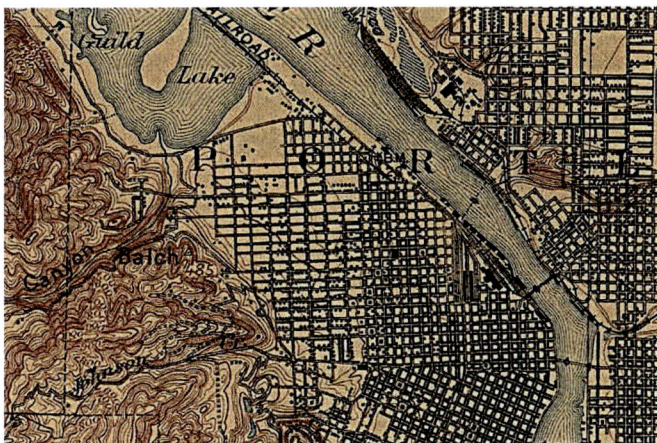

*NW Portland in 1897, at the end of our story. Guild's Lake was still there, soon to host the 1905 Lewis & Clark Exposition. Union Station had by then replaced Couch Lake. Just before the Great Renaming of 1891, Albina and East Portland were absorbed into the city. Portland was ready for a new century.*[4]

# NOTES

## INTRODUCTION

1. Carl Abbott, *Portland in Three Centuries: The Place and the People* (Corvallis: Oregon State University Press, 2011), 16. http://osupress.oregonstate.edu/sites/default/files/ Abbott.PortlandinThreeCenturies.excerpt.pdf, accessed June 5, 2016.
2. Percy Maddux, *City on the Willamette* (Portland: Metropolitan Press, 1952), 24.
3. Richard Marlitt, *Nineteenth Street*, (Portland: Oregon Historical Society, 1978).
4. E. Kimbark MacColl, *The Shaping of a City* (Portland: The Georgian Press Company, 1976), 5. (Frankfurt, Germany, and Hartford, Connecticut, were the first and second wealthiest cities in the world.)
5. Eugene Snyder, *Portland Names and Neighborhoods.* (Portland: Binford & Mort, 1979), 53.
6. Snyder, *Portland Names*, 54.
7. Snyder, *Portland Names*, 55.
8. www.portlandoregon.gov/bps/article/149586.
9. www.portlandoregon.gov/bps/article/149586.
10. City of Portland Archives, Oregon, 7263 - Providing for the change of the names of Certain Streets in the City of Portland, Record Series 2001-07, 12/30/1891.

## A

1. The Southern Oregon Historical Society, "The Table Rock Sentinel," *The Ankeny Years*, in "Sunrise to Sunset at Sterlingville," March 1982, 11.
2. Portland's Skidmore Fountain, http://www.skidmoremarket.com/ under New Market Block, accessed May 2, 2016.
3. *The Ankeny Years*, 11.
4. Snyder, *Portland Names*, 88. Snyder gives an interesting and detailed accounting of the reasons for this narrow street called Ankeny.
5. http://www.saturdaymarket.com/, accessed May 2, 2016.

## B

1. Snyder, *Portland Names*, 103.
2. Rebecca Koffman, "The Future of Old Chinatown," *The Oregonian*, March 11, 2014.
3. Snyder, *Portland Names*, 103.

## C

1. Joseph Gaston, *The Centennial History of Oregon, 1811–1912, Vol. I*, (Chicago: The S. J. Clarke Publishing Company, 1912), 373.
2. Joseph Gaston, *Portland, Its History and Builders, Vol. II*, (Chicago: The S. J. Clarke Publishing Company, 1911), 375.
3. Snyder, *Portland Names*, 26.
4. Couch house photo, Oregon Historical Society, bb014237
5. William J. Hawkins III & William F. Willingham, *Classic Houses of Portland, Oregon*, (Portland, Oregon: Timber Press, 1999), 42.
6. National Park Service, Department of the Interior, "Balfour–Guthrie Building," Section 8, page 2, 8/1/02. The conversation actually took place in 1877 when the new manager of Balfour and Guthrie, Mr. Walter Burns, asked how to succeed in Portland. http://focus.nps.gov/pdfhost/docs/NRHP/Text/02000824.pdf, accessed June 6, 2016. *Note:* MacColl, *Shaping of a City*, n. 53 identifies George Weidler as the one offering the advice. For additional evidence of Couch as a 'founding father," MacColl calculates that besides his 4 daughters, the Captain had "22 grandchildren, and 33 great-grandchildren." MacColl, *Shaping*, n. 27.

7. Captain John Couch and his wife Caroline photo, Oregon Historical Society, bb004081.
8. Snyder, *Portland Names*, 29.
9. "Sketches of Oregon," *The Morning Oregonian*, January 25, 1870, 1. http://0-phw01.newsbank.com.catalog.multcolib.org/cache/ean/fullsize/pl_006112016_1736_03114_41.pdf, accessed June 6, 2016.

**D**

1. Harvey Scott, *History of Portland, Oregon*, (Syracuse: D. Mason and Company, 1890), 381.
2. E. Kimbark MacColl, *Merchants, Money, and Power: The Portland Establishment, 1843–1913*, (University of Michigan: Georgian Press, 1988), 110.
3. T. H. Crawford, *Historical Sketch of the Public Schools of Portland, Oregon, 1847–1888*, 4. http://www.pps.net/site/handlers/filedownload.ashx?moduleinstanceid=344&dataid=413&FileName=Historical-Sketch-PPS.pdf, accessed June 6, 2016.

**E**

1. *Wikipedia*, "Lovejoy Columns."
2. *The Oregonian*, Everett, October 14, 1921, 12. http://0-phw02.newsbank.com.catalog.multcolib.org/cache/ean/fullsize/pl_006112016_2112_30184_998.pdf, accessed June 10, 2016.
3. *The Oregonian*, Everett, October 14, 1921, 12.

**F**

1. https://www.portlandoregon.gov/bps/article/146291, accessed May 21, 2016.
2. Snyder, *Portland Names*, 130.
3. Snyder, *Stumptown Triumphant*, 44–45.
4. Northwest District Association *Northwest Portland Historic Inventory, Historic Context Statement, 1991*, 14. Along with brother-in-law Flanders, other members of the Couch clan who moved to 19th Street included son-in-law Cicero Lewis and sons-in-law Dr. Rodney Glisan and Dr. Robert Wilson. http://www.oregon.gov/oprd/HCD/OHC/docs/multnomah_portland_northwest_historiccontext_vol1.pdf, accessed May 21, 2016. *Note:* Richard Marlitt, *Nineteenth Street* (Portland: Oregon Historical Society, 1978). This book is a revealing look at some of these mansions, inside and out. Much of the book is dedicated to houses owned by the extended Couch family.
5. www.orhf.org/oregon-rail-heritage-center/our-locomotives/sp-4449/, accessed May 21, 2016.
6. Joseph Gaston, *Portland: Its History and Builders Vol. I*, (Chicago–Portland: The S.J. Clarke Publishing Co., 1911), 214. *Note:* Jewel Lansing, *Portland: People, Politics, and Power 1851–2001*, (Corvallis: Oregon State University Press, 2003), 139. Lansing contends that the East Side might very well have been the business hub of Portland had the fund drive for Union Station not been successful.
7. "An Old Settler Dying," *The Sunday Oregonian*, November 20, 1892. http://0-infoweb.newsbank.com.catalog.multcolib.org/resources/doc/nb/image/, accessed May 21, 2016.
8. Gaston, *Portland: Its History and Builders Vol. II*, (Chicago–Portland: The S. J. Clarke Publishing Co., 1911), 522.

**G**

1. *Wikipedia*, "Rodney Glisan." https://en.wikipedia.org/wiki/Rodney_Glisan, accessed June 2, 2016.
2. Dr. Rodney Glisan (1827–1890). Olof Larsell Papers, OHSU Historical Collections & Archives, Portland, Oregon.

3. *Wikipedia*, "Rodney Glisan."

4. "Death of Dr. Rodney Glisan," *The Morning Oregonian*, June 4, 1890, 6, http://0-phw02.newsbank.com.catalog.multcolib.org/cache/ean/fullsize/pl_006112016_2137_43450_220.pdf, accessed June 2, 2016.

5. *Wikipedia*, "Rodney Glisan."

6. Certificate photo courtesy of Multnomah County Library. Multnomah County Library Membership for Dr. Rodney Glisan, https://gallery.multcolib.org/image/certificate-perpetual-membership-no-4-dr-rodney-glisan, accessed June 2, 2016.

**H**

1. James D. Miller, "Early Oregon Scenes: A Pioneer Narrative, Vol. II," in *Oregon Historical Quarterly* 31, no. 2 (June, 1930), 160–180. Portland: Oregon Historical Society, http://www.jstor.org/stable/20610551, accessed June 5, 2016.

2. Snyder, *Portland Names*, 131.

3. *Wikipedia*, poet signed "O.P.Q." in *Oregon Spectator*, August 19, 1851. As quoted in Mills, *Sternwheelers up Columbia* (Pacific Books, 1947), 22. https://en.wikipedia.org/wiki/Multnomah_%28sidewheeler_1851%29, accessed June 8, 2016.

4. *Wikipedia*, "Steamboats of the Columbia River." Date and location of photograph established from Wright, ed., Lewis and Dryden Marine History, 34. https://en.wikipedia.org/wiki/Multnomah_%28sidewheeler_1851%29, accessed June 8, 2016.

5. Lone Fir Cemetery Grave Marker. http://www.findagrave.com/cgi-bin/fg.cgi?page=gr&GRid=59319741, accessed May 24, 2016.

**I**

1. *Wikipedia*, "Couch Family Investment Development," https://en.wikipedia.org/wiki/File:Couch_Family_Investment_Development_no3_-_Portland_Oregon.jpg, accessed May 17, 2016.

2. *Wikipedia*, "Steamboats of the Columbia River," https://en.wikipedia.org/wiki/Steamboats_of_the_Columbia_River, accessed May 15, 2016.

3. Snyder, *Portland Names*, 155.

4. *Wikipedia*, "William Irving (Steamship Captain)," https://en.wikipedia.org/wiki/William_Irving_%28steamship_captain%29, accessed May 4, 2016.

**J**

1. Snyder, *Portland Names*, 157. *Note:* See Mike Ryerson, Norm Gholston, and Tracy J. Prince, *Portland's Slabtown* (Charleston: Arcadia Publishing, 2013) for more history and photographs of these creeks.

2. Scott, *History of Portland*, 563.

3. Classified Ad, *The Oregonian*, August 26, 1876.

4. The City of Portland, "King's Hill Historic District Guidelines," 116. https://www.portlandoregon.gov/bps/article/58856, accessed May 26, 2016.

5. The City of Portland, "Kings Hill," 111. https://www.portlandoregon.gov/bps/article/58856, accessed May 26, 2016.

**K**

1. http://www.usmarshals.gov/readingroom/us_marshals/oregon.pdf, accessed June 4, 2016. http://www.historylink.org/index.cfm?DisplayPage=output.cfm&file_id=essay5238, accessed June 4, 2016.

2. Snyder, *Portland Names*, 158.

3. *The Morning Oregonian*, October 19, 1921, 13. http://0-phw02.newsbank.com.catalog.multcolib.org/cache/ean/fullsize/pl_006112016_1739_45726_526.pdf, accessed June 4, 2016

4. *The Morning Oregonian* (October 19, 1921), 13.

5. *Encyclopedia of Washington State History*, "McNeil Island and the Federal Penitentiary, 1841–1981." http://www.historylink.org/index.cfm?DisplayPage=output.cfm&file_id=5238, accessed June 8, 2016.

## PORTLAND & "THE SIMPSONS" CONNECTION

1. Scott Cook and Aimee Wade, *PDXccentric—The Odyssey of Portland Oddities* (Slough Biscuit Press, 2014), 93.

2. "Top 10 Best Ned Flanders Quotes," #5, #2, http://www.top10-best.com/n/top_10_best_ned_flanders_quotes.html, accessed April 7, 2016.

3. http://simpsons.wikia.com/wiki/Kearney_Zzyzwicz, accessed April 7, 2016. Author's update, November 2016: Will Kearney stop being a bully now that the Cubs are World Series champions!?

4. https://escapetoreality.org/2010/04/01/christianity-in-the-simpsons-top-12-reverend-lovejoy-quotes/, accessed April 7, 2016.

5. "The Eighteenth Amendment, Quotes," http://simpsons.wikia.com/wiki/Homer_vs._the_Eighteenth_Amendment/Quotes, accessed April 8, 2016.

### L

1. The coin is now displayed in the lobby of the Oregon Historical Society. The elapsed years have spawned numerous versions of this famous coin toss. The most comprehensive collection of these tales can be found at the informative Dan Haneckow blog, *Café Unknown.com* under the heading "The Vexed Question." In a much earlier article in the *Oregon Native Son* magazine, "Portland Oregon, Its Founders and Early Businessmen," the writer is quoted as saying that this Matron Head penny was "no doubt then the only one in Oregon." *The Oregon Native Son*, Vol. II, 1901, 331. https://books.google.com/books?id=N8AUAAAAYAAJ&dq=The+Oregon+native+son+1901&source=gbs_navlinks_s, accessed June 7, 2016.

2. Shawn O'bryant, *Willamette Week*, May 5, 2009, Lovejoy, Stamps of Approval. http://www.wweek.com/portland/article-10491-stamps-of-approval.html, accessed April 8, 2016.

3. Asa Lovejoy photo, Oregon Historical Society, #bb000666.

### M

1. Snyder, *Portland Names*, 176. As quoted in Marshall, *The Morning Oregonian*, October 26, 1921, 13. http://0-phw02.newsbank.com.catalog.multcolib.org/cache/ean/fullsize/pl_006112016_1744_23925_800.pdf, accessed May 22, 2016.

2. *Wikipedia* (January 1, 2014), quoted in *The Oregonian*, October 26, 1921, 13.

3. *The Morning Oregonian* August 23, 1921, 20. http://0-phw01.newsbank.com.catalog.multcolib.org/cache/ean/fullsize/pl_006112016_2102_39800_459.pdf, accessed June 5, 2016.

4. Gaston, *Portland, Oregon, Vol. II*, 776.

5. *The Morning Oregonian*, August 23, 1921.

### N

1. Edward J. Northrup, rootsweb.ancestry.com, http://www.rootsweb.ancestry.com/~ormultno/History/Scott/biogM-S/northrup.htm, accessed May 2, 2016.

2. *The Morning Oregonian*, July 25, 1878 2. http://0-infoweb.newsbank.com.catalog.multcolib.org/resources/doc/nb/image/v2%3A11A73E5827618330%40EANX-NB-12349AC92F7FBAA0%402407191-122FAC25733C3218%401-12D4BB65C2E8A100%40No%2BHeadline?p=AMNEWS, accessed June 5, 2016.

3. *Oregon Native Son, Vol. II*, "Edward J. Northrup," May 1900, 45.
4. Edward J. Northrup photo, http://www.findagrave.com/cgi-bin/fg.cgi?page=pv&GR id=52226550&PIpi=90259423, accessed June 8, 2016.
5. Scott, *History of Portland*, 624.
6. U.S. Department of the Interior, "National Register of Historic Places Inventory," 8. http://focus.nps.gov/GetAsset?assetID=09b33739-87db-4916-bf3b-dd55fe603294, accessed June 8, 2016.

**O**

1. "One History Sleuth's Radical Theory: Everything We Know About How Portland Began Is Wrong," *Portland Monthly*, Leah Sottile, May 19, 2016. http://www.pdx-monthly.com/articles/2016/5/19/one-history-sleuth-s-radical-theory-everything-we-know-about-how-portland-began-is-wrong, accessed July 9, 2016.
2. Senator J. W. Nesmith, "Oregon Pioneer Association Transactions for 1875," 57. https://archive.org/stream/OregonPioneerAssociationTransactionsFor1875/75-OPA-Transactions-03_djvu.txt, accessed April 4, 2016.
3. Scott, *History of Portland*, Oregon, 81.
4. T. T. Geer, *Fifty Years in Oregon* (The Neale Publishing Co., 1912). Chapter XIX, Diary entry February 24, 1848. http://www.theragens.com/fifty_years/fifty_years_in_oregon_18-19.htm, accessed April 4, 2016.
5. Portland 1851, Oregon Historical Society, bb014236

**P**

1. Francis Pettygrove photo, Oregon Historical Society, bb002972.
2. MacColl, *Merchants, Money and Power*, 10.
3. MacColl, *Merchants, Money and Power*, 11.
4. Daniel Lownsdale deserves mention here in the story of early Portland even though his name is not on an alphabet street. It has been noted that his tannery was a great boon to the development of commerce in early Portland. Tanner Creek, on which he built his business, runs (now underground) through Northwest Portland. His contribution is celebrated at Tanner Springs Park, NW 10th Avenue and Marshall, just before the creek empties into the Willamette River.

**Q**

1. *Portrait and Biographical Record of the Willamette Valley, Oregon* (Chicago, Chapman Publishing Co., 1903), 185.
2. U.S. Department of the Interior, Skidmore/Old Town Historic District, 47, https://www.nps.gov/nhl/apply/pdfs/Criterion5_Skidmore.pdf, accessed May 27, 2016. *Note:* In 1873, Portland had one liquor outlet for every 205 people. By loose comparison, LaCrosse, Wisconsin, which has more bars per person than any other US city today, has only 0.14 bars for every 205 people. http://247wallst.com/special-report/2016/05/14/the-drunkest-and-driest-cities-in-america/4/, accessed June 5, 2016.
3. *The Morning Oregonian*, April 26, 1907, 9.
4. Louise Swan, "Perkins decided to build a new hotel," as quoted in *Northwest Magazine*, May 3, 1981, 7. https://vintageportland.files.wordpress.com/2011/04/perkins-hotel-19810503a.pdf, accessed June 5, 2016.
5. http://www.wweek.com/portland/article-10491-stamps-of-approval.html, accessed June 5, 2016.
6. *The Oregonian*, October 24, 1921, 6. http://0-phw02.newsbank.com.catalog.mult-colib.org/cache/ean/fullsize/pl_006112016_2024_59154_265.pdf, accessed June 5, 2016.

7. Portland Archives and Record Center (PARC), 1886 Directory, Box Number 2616, A2012-030.

**R**

1. Snyder, *Portland Names*, 193.
2. Oregon Blue Book, "List of Employees in Custom Service, Port of Portland, Oregon, District of Willamette," 185. https://books.google.com/books?id=LD00AQAAMA AJ&dq=A.E.+raleigh+portland&source=gbs_navlinks_s, accessed April 2, 2016.
3. *The Morning Oregonian*, November 19, 1895, 5. http://0-phw02.newsbank.com.catalog.multcolib.org/cache/ean/fullsize/pl_006112016_1840_25549_216.pdf, accessed May 25, 2016.
4. Ryerson, Gholston, Prince, *Portland's Slabtown*, 14–15.
5. *Wikipedia*, "Chinook Jargon." https://en.wikipedia.org/wiki/Chinook_Jargon#/media/File:Gill%27s_Dictionary_of_the_Chinook_Jargon_01B.jpg, accessed June 5, 2016.

**S**

1. City of Portland Archives, Oregon, A2004-002.
2. Gaston, *History of Portland Vol.II*, 593.
3. City of Portland Archives, Oregon, 7373 Changing the Name of Scott St. to Savier St., Record Series 2001-07, 02/05/1892.
4. *NW Examiner*, February 2016, 4.

**T**

1. Snyder, *Portland Names*, 213.
2. *The Oregonian*, October 28, 1921, 13. http://0-phw01.newsbank.com.catalog.multcolib.org/cache/ean/fullsize/pl_006112016_2031_03572_737.pdf, accessed June 5, 2016.
3. See Donald Nelson's book, *Sons of Slabtown & Tales of Westside Sports*, Portland, Oregon, 2016. You will find a wealth of information about Slabtown here, especially its sports figures.

**U**

1. Snyder, *Portland Names*, 221.
2. *Wikipedia*, Portrait by A. G. Heaton, https://en.wikipedia.org/wiki/Abel_P._Upshur, accessed June 5, 2016.
3. Ann Blackman, "Fatal Cruise of the Princeton" in *Navy History*, September, 2005. http://www.military.com/NewContent/0,13190,NH_0905_Cruise-P1,00.html, accessed May 29, 2016.
4. *Wikipedia*, "The USS Princeton disaster of 1844." https://en.wikipedia.org/wiki/USS_Princeton_disaster_of_1844#/media/File:Explosion_aboard_USS_Princeton.jpg, N. Currier (firm) - Library of Congress, Prints & Photographs Division, LC-USZC2-3201 (color film copy slide), archival TIFF version (4 MB), accessed June 5, 2016.

**V**

1. Dan Haneckow, *Café Unknown*. http://www.cafeunknown.com/2007/11/city-in-flames-london-chicago-san.html, accessed April 20, 2016. The blog is full of history and photographs of this major fire.
2. *The Oregonian* Monday, August 4, 1873, 4. http://0-phw02.newsbank.com.catalog.multcolib.org/cache/ean/fullsize/pl_006112016_1844_27571_977.pdf, accessed June 5, 2016.
3. MacColl, *Merchants, Money, and Power*, 175.

4. *The Oregonian*, October 29, 1921, 12. http://0-phw01.newsbank.com.catalog.mult-colib.org/cache/ean/fullsize/pl_006112016_2041_29226_536.pdf, accessed June 9, 2016.
5. PdxHistory.com, "Portland Baseball." http://www.pdxhistory.com/html/portland_baseball.html, accessed June 5, 2016.

**W**

1. Gaston, *Portland, Its History and Builders, Vol.III*, 16.
2. Lansing, *Portland*, 61.
3. "History of the OHSU Library," http://www.ohsu.edu/xd/education/library/about/collections/historical-collections-archives/about/histoflibshort.cfm, accessed June 5, 2016.
4. Dr. R. B. Wilson (1828–1887). Olof Larsell Papers, OHSU Historical Collections & Archives, Portland, Oregon.
5. Willamette Medical Department, 15th and Couch Street, erected 1889. Olof Larsell Papers, OHSU Historical Collections & Archives, Portland, Oregon.
6. *Oregon Native Son*, Vol I, 404.

**Y**

1. *The Skanner*, May 22, 2002, Portland, Oregon, Volume XXVII, No. 34.
2. City of Portland, Vera Katz, Mayor, Resolution 36070, May 22, 2002.
3. Fred Leeson, "Portland Street now named for black explorer" in *The Oregonian*, May 23, 2002. http://0-infoweb.newsbank.com.catalog.multcolib.org/resources/doc/nb/news/0F3BA0A343F2ABEF?p=AMNEWS, accessed October 29, 2016.
4. Robert B. Betts, *In Search of York*, (University Press of Colorado, 1985), p. 41.
5. Steve Beaven, *The Oregonian*, May 8, 2010. http://www.oregonlive.com/news/index.ssf/2010/05/statue_at_lewis_clark_college.html, accessed October 29, 2016.
6. Fred Leeson, *The Oregonian*, May 23, 2002.
7. Fred Leeson, *The Oregonian*, May 23, 2002.
8. Carl Abbott, *The Great Extravaganza*, Portland and the Lewis and Clark Exposition, (Portland: Oregon Historical Society, 2004), 59.
9. *Wikipedia*, "Lewis and Clark Centennial Exposition and Records Center." https://en.wikipedia.org/wiki/Lewis_and_Clark_Centennial_Exposition, accessed June 5, 2016.

**POSTSCRIPT**

1. "Alphabet District Street Names," http://www.portlandhometeam.com/alphabet-district-street-names.php, accessed June 5, 2016.
2. Abbott, *The Great Extravaganza*, 3 (facing).
3. Facts About Reed, "Mission and History," https://www.reed.edu/about_reed/history.html, accessed June 5, 2016.
4. 1897 Map of Portland, https://www.lib.utexas.edu/maps/historical/portland_or_1897.jpg, accessed June 5, 2016.

# BIBLIOGRAPHY

Abbott, Carl. *The Great Extravaganza*. Portland: Oregon Historical Society, 2004.

Betts, Robert B., *In Search of York*. University Press of Colorado and the Lewis and Clark Trail Heritage Foundation, 1985.

Blalock, Barney. *Portland's Lost Waterfront*. Charleston: The History Press, 2012.

Comerford, Jane. *A History of Northwest Portland: From the River to the Hills*. Portland: Dragonfly Press, 2011.

Gaston, Joseph. *Portland, Its History and Builders, Vols. I, II, III*. Chicago: The S. J. Clarke Publishing Company, 1911.

Gorseck, Christopher S. *Portland's Pearl District*. Charleston: Arcadia Publishing, 2012.

Harrison, Rebecca and Daniel Cowan. *Portland's Maritime History*. Charleston: Arcadia Publishing, 2014.

Hawkins, William John III. *The Grand Era of Cast Iron Architecture in Portland*. Portland: Binford & Mort Publishers, 1976.

Hawkins, William J. III and William F. Willingham. *Classic Houses of Portland, Oregon 1850–1950*. Portland: Timber Press, Inc., 2005.

Lansing, Jewel. *Portland People, Politics, and Power 1851–2001*. Corvallis, Oregon: Oregon State University Press, 2005.

Larsell, O. *The Doctor in Oregon*. Portland: Binfords & Mort for the Oregon Historical Society, 1947.

MacColl, E. Kimbark. *Merchants, Money and Power*. Portland: The Georgian Press Company, 1988.

MacColl, E. Kimbark. *The Shaping of a City*. Portland: The Georgian Press Company, 1976.

Maddux, Percy. *City on the Willamette*. Portland: Metropolitan Press, 1952.

Marschner, Janice. Oregon 1859, *A Snapshot in Time*. Portland: Timber Press, 2009.

Marlitt, Richard. *Nineteenth Street*. Portland: Oregon Historical Society, 1978.

Ryerson, Mike, Norm Gholston, and Tracy J. Prince. *Portland's Stabtown*. Charleston: Arcadia Publishing, 2013.

Scott, Harvey. *History of Portland, Oregon*. Syracuse: D. Mason & Co., 1890.

Snyder, Eugene E. *Early Portland: Stump-Town Triumphant 1831–1854*. Portland: Binford & Mort, 1970.

Snyder, Eugene E. *Portland Names and Neighborhoods: Their Historic Origins*. Portland, Binford & Mort, 1979.

**OTHER RESOURCES**

Dan Haneckow, *Café Unknown*, blog

*findagrave.com* (online)

Multnomah County Library

Portland Archives and Records Center (PARC)

OHSU Historical Collections and Archives

Oregon Historical Society

*Portland Monthly*

*Portland Tribune*

*The Morning Oregonian* (online)

*The NW Examiner*

*The Oregonian* (online)

*Wikipedia* (online)